Trips Journal

Travel Journal for Kids

This Journal Belongs To

_____

Age: _____

Date of my Trip: _____/_____/_____   Place: _____

Picture of the Day

Details
Write about what you did, the best part of the day, what you saw, your favorite part of the day, what you liked or didn't like or anything else interesting.

Date of my Trip: _____/_____/_____ Place: _____

Picture of the Day

Details
Write about what you did, the best part of the day, what you saw, your favorite part of the day, what you liked or didn't like or anything else interesting.

Date of my Trip: _____/_____/_____   Place: _____

Picture of the Day

Details
Write about what you did, the best part of the day, what you saw, your favorite part of the day, what you liked or didn't like or anything else interesting.

_____

_____

_____

_____

_____

_____

_____

_____

_____

_____

_____

_____

Date of my Trip: _____/_____/_____   Place: _____

Picture of the Day

Details
Write about what you did, the best part of the day, what you saw, your favorite part of the day, what you liked or didn't like or anything else interesting.

Date of my Trip: _____/_____/_____   Place: _____

Picture of the Day

Details
Write about what you did, the best part of the day, what you saw, your favorite part of the day, what you liked or didn't like or anything else interesting.

Date of my Trip: _____/_____/_____   Place: _____

Picture of the Day

Details
Write about what you did, the best part of the day, what you saw, your favorite part of the day, what you liked or didn't like or anything else interesting.

- -

- -

- -

- -

- -

- -

- -

- -

- -

- -

- -

- -

Date of my Trip: _____/_____/_____   Place: _____

Picture of the Day

Details
Write about what you did, the best part of the day, what you saw, your favorite part of the day, what you liked or didn't like or anything else interesting.

_____

_____

_____

_____

_____

_____

_____

_____

_____

_____

_____

_____

Date of my Trip: _____/_____/_____   Place: _____

Picture of the Day

Details

Write about what you did, the best part of the day, what you saw, your favorite part of the day, what you liked or didn't like or anything else interesting.

Date of my Trip: _____/_____/_____   Place: _____

Picture of the Day

Details
Write about what you did, the best part of the day, what you saw, your favorite part of the day, what you liked or didn't like or anything else interesting.

- -

- -

- -

- -

- -

- -

- -

- -

- -

- -

- -

- -

Date of my Trip: _____/_____/_____ Place: _____

Picture of the Day

Details
Write about what you did, the best part of the day, what you saw, your favorite part of the day, what you liked or didn't like or anything else interesting.

Date of my Trip: _____/_____/_____   Place: _____

Picture of the Day

Details

Write about what you did, the best part of the day, what you saw, your favorite part of the day, what you liked or didn't like or anything else interesting.

- -

- -

- -

- -

- -

- -

- -

- -

- -

- -

- -

- -

Date of my Trip: _____/_____/_____   Place: _____

Picture of the Day

Details
Write about what you did, the best part of the day, what you saw, your favorite part of the day, what you liked or didn't like or anything else interesting.

Date of my Trip: _____/_____/_____   Place: _____

Picture of the Day

Details
Write about what you did, the best part of the day, what you saw, your favorite part of the day, what you liked or didn't like or anything else interesting.

Date of my Trip: _____/_____/_____   Place: _____

Picture of the Day

Details
Write about what you did, the best part of the day, what you saw, your favorite part of the day, what you liked or didn't like or anything else interesting.

Date of my Trip: _____/_____/_____ Place: _____

Picture of the Day

Details
Write about what you did, the best part of the day, what you saw, your favorite part of the day, what you liked or didn't like or anything else interesting.

Date of my Trip: _____/_____/_____   Place: _____

Picture of the Day

Details
Write about what you did, the best part of the day, what you saw, your favorite part of the day, what you liked or didn't like or anything else interesting.

- -

- -

- -

- -

- -

- -

- -

- -

- -

- -

- -

Date of my Trip: _____/_____/_____ Place: _____

Picture of the Day

Details
Write about what you did, the best part of the day, what you saw, your favorite part of the day, what you liked or didn't like or anything else interesting.

Date of my Trip: _____/_____/_____   Place: _____

Picture of the Day

Details
Write about what you did, the best part of the day, what you saw, your favorite part of the day, what you liked or didn't like or anything else interesting.

- -

- -

- -

- -

- -

- -

- -

- -

- -

- -

- -

- -

Date of my Trip: _____/_____/_____   Place: _____

Picture of the Day

Details
Write about what you did, the best part of the day, what you saw, your favorite part of the day, what you liked or didn't like or anything else interesting.

- -

- -

- -

- -

- -

- -

- -

- -

- -

- -

- -

- -

Date of my Trip: _____/_____/_____   Place: _____

Picture of the Day

Details
Write about what you did, the best part of the day, what you saw, your favorite part of the day, what you liked or didn't like or anything else interesting.

- -

- -

- -

- -

- -

- -

- -

- -

- -

- -

- -

- -

Date of my Trip: _____/_____/_____   Place: _____

Picture of the Day

Details
Write about what you did, the best part of the day, what you saw, your favorite part of the day, what you liked or didn't like or anything else interesting.

Date of my Trip: _____/_____/_____   Place: _____

Picture of the Day

Details
Write about what you did, the best part of the day, what you saw, your favorite
part of the day, what you liked or didn't like or anything else interesting.

Date of my Trip: _____/_____/_____   Place: _____

Picture of the Day

Details
Write about what you did, the best part of the day, what you saw, your favorite part of the day, what you liked or didn't like or anything else interesting.

Date of my Trip: _____ / _____ / _____   Place: _____

Picture of the Day

Details
Write about what you did, the best part of the day, what you saw, your favorite part of the day, what you liked or didn't like or anything else interesting.

Date of my Trip: _____/_____/_____   Place: _____

Picture of the Day

Details
Write about what you did, the best part of the day, what you saw, your favorite part of the day, what you liked or didn't like or anything else interesting.

Date of my Trip: _____/_____/_____   Place: _____

Picture of the Day

Details
Write about what you did, the best part of the day, what you saw, your favorite part of the day, what you liked or didn't like or anything else interesting.

Date of my Trip: _____/_____/_____   Place: _____

Picture of the Day

Details
Write about what you did, the best part of the day, what you saw, your favorite part of the day, what you liked or didn't like or anything else interesting.

_____

_____

_____

_____

_____

_____

_____

_____

_____

_____

_____

_____

_____

Date of my Trip: _____/_____/_____   Place: _____

Picture of the Day

Details
Write about what you did, the best part of the day, what you saw, your favorite part of the day, what you liked or didn't like or anything else interesting.

Date of my Trip: _____/_____/_____ Place: _____

Picture of the Day

Details
Write about what you did, the best part of the day, what you saw, your favorite part of the day, what you liked or didn't like or anything else interesting.

Date of my Trip: _____/_____/_____   Place: _____

Picture of the Day

Details
Write about what you did, the best part of the day, what you saw, your favorite part of the day, what you liked or didn't like or anything else interesting.

Date of my Trip: _____/_____/_____ Place: _____

Picture of the Day

Details
Write about what you did, the best part of the day, what you saw, your favorite part of the day, what you liked or didn't like or anything else interesting.

_____

_____

_____

_____

_____

_____

_____

_____

_____

_____

_____

_____

_____

Date of my Trip: _____/_____/_____ Place: _____

Picture of the Day

Details
Write about what you did, the best part of the day, what you saw, your favorite part of the day, what you liked or didn't like or anything else interesting.

Date of my Trip: _____/_____/_____   Place: _____

Picture of the Day

Details
Write about what you did, the best part of the day, what you saw, your favorite part of the day, what you liked or didn't like or anything else interesting.

_____

_____

_____

_____

_____

_____

_____

_____

_____

_____

_____

_____

Date of my Trip: _____/_____/_____   Place: _____

Picture of the Day

Details
Write about what you did, the best part of the day, what you saw, your favorite part of the day, what you liked or didn't like or anything else interesting.

- -

- -

- -

- -

- -

- -

- -

- -

- -

- -

- -

- -

Date of my Trip: _____/_____/_____   Place: _____

Picture of the Day

Details
Write about what you did, the best part of the day, what you saw, your favorite part of the day, what you liked or didn't like or anything else interesting.

Date of my Trip: _____/_____/_____   Place: _____

Picture of the Day

Details
Write about what you did, the best part of the day, what you saw, your favorite part of the day, what you liked or didn't like or anything else interesting.

- -
- -
- -
- -
- -
- -
- -
- -
- -
- -
- -

Date of my Trip: _____/_____/_____ Place: _____

Picture of the Day

Details

Write about what you did, the best part of the day, what you saw, your favorite part of the day, what you liked or didn't like or anything else interesting.

Date of my Trip: _____/_____/_____   Place: _____

Picture of the Day

Details
Write about what you did, the best part of the day, what you saw, your favorite part of the day, what you liked or didn't like or anything else interesting.

- -

- -

- -

- -

- -

- -

- -

- -

- -

- -

- -

- -

Date of my Trip: _____/_____/_____ Place: _____

Picture of the Day

Details

Write about what you did, the best part of the day, what you saw, your favorite part of the day, what you liked or didn't like or anything else interesting.

- -

- -

- -

- -

- -

- -

- -

- -

- -

- -

- -

- -

- -

Date of my Trip: _____/_____/_____   Place: _____

Picture of the Day

Details

Write about what you did, the best part of the day, what you saw, your favorite part of the day, what you liked or didn't like or anything else interesting.

- -

- -

- -

- -

- -

- -

- -

- -

- -

- -

- -

Date of my Trip: _____/_____/_____   Place: _____

Picture of the Day

Details
Write about what you did, the best part of the day, what you saw, your favorite part of the day, what you liked or didn't like or anything else interesting.

_____

_____

_____

_____

_____

_____

_____

_____

_____

_____

_____

_____

Date of my Trip: _____/_____/_____   Place: _____

Picture of the Day

Details
Write about what you did, the best part of the day, what you saw, your favorite part of the day, what you liked or didn't like or anything else interesting.

Date of my Trip: _____/_____/_____   Place: _____

Picture of the Day

Details
Write about what you did, the best part of the day, what you saw, your favorite part of the day, what you liked or didn't like or anything else interesting.

- -

- -

- -

- -

- -

- -

- -

- -

- -

- -

- -

- -

Date of my Trip: _____/_____/_____   Place: _____

Picture of the Day

Details

Write about what you did, the best part of the day, what you saw, your favorite part of the day, what you liked or didn't like or anything else interesting.

Date of my Trip: _____/_____/_____ Place: _____

Picture of the Day

Details
Write about what you did, the best part of the day, what you saw, your favorite part of the day, what you liked or didn't like or anything else interesting.

Date of my Trip: _____/_____/_____   Place: _____

Picture of the Day

Details
Write about what you did, the best part of the day, what you saw, your favorite part of the day, what you liked or didn't like or anything else interesting.

Date of my Trip: _____/_____/_____   Place: _____

Picture of the Day

Details
Write about what you did, the best part of the day, what you saw, your favorite part of the day, what you liked or didn't like or anything else interesting.

Date of my Trip: _____/_____/_____ Place: _____

Picture of the Day

Details
Write about what you did, the best part of the day, what you saw, your favorite part of the day, what you liked or didn't like or anything else interesting.

Date of my Trip: _____/_____/_____   Place: _____

Picture of the Day

Details
Write about what you did, the best part of the day, what you saw, your favorite part of the day, what you liked or didn't like or anything else interesting.

_____

_____

_____

_____

_____

_____

_____

_____

_____

_____

_____

_____

Date of my Trip: _____/_____/_____   Place: _____

Picture of the Day

Details
Write about what you did, the best part of the day, what you saw, your favorite part of the day, what you liked or didn't like or anything else interesting.

Date of my Trip: _____/_____/_____   Place: _____

Picture of the Day

Details
Write about what you did, the best part of the day, what you saw, your favorite part of the day, what you liked or didn't like or anything else interesting.

Date of my Trip: _____/_____/_____   Place: _____

Picture of the Day

Details
Write about what you did, the best part of the day, what you saw, your favorite part of the day, what you liked or didn't like or anything else interesting.

Date of my Trip: _____/_____/_____   Place: _____

Picture of the Day

Details
Write about what you did, the best part of the day, what you saw, your favorite part of the day, what you liked or didn't like or anything else interesting.

_____

_____

_____

_____

_____

_____

_____

_____

_____

_____

_____

_____

Date of my Trip: _____/_____/_____   Place: _____

Picture of the Day

Details
Write about what you did, the best part of the day, what you saw, your favorite part of the day, what you liked or didn't like or anything else interesting.

Date of my Trip: _____/_____/_____ Place: _____

Picture of the Day

Details
Write about what you did, the best part of the day, what you saw, your favorite part of the day, what you liked or didn't like or anything else interesting.

_____

_____

_____

_____

_____

_____

_____

_____

_____

_____

_____

_____

Date of my Trip: _____/_____/_____   Place: _____

Picture of the Day

Details
Write about what you did, the best part of the day, what you saw, your favorite part of the day, what you liked or didn't like or anything else interesting.

Date of my Trip: _____/_____/_____ Place: _____

Picture of the Day

Details
Write about what you did, the best part of the day, what you saw, your favorite part of the day, what you liked or didn't like or anything else interesting.

_____

_____

_____

_____

_____

_____

_____

_____

_____

_____

_____

_____

Date of my Trip: _____/_____/_____   Place: _____

Picture of the Day

Details
Write about what you did, the best part of the day, what you saw, your favorite part of the day, what you liked or didn't like or anything else interesting.

Date of my Trip: _____/_____/_____   Place: _____

Picture of the Day

Details
Write about what you did, the best part of the day, what you saw, your favorite part of the day, what you liked or didn't like or anything else interesting.

_____

_____

_____

_____

_____

_____

_____

_____

_____

_____

_____

Date of my Trip: _____/_____/_____   Place: _____

Picture of the Day

Details
Write about what you did, the best part of the day, what you saw, your favorite part of the day, what you liked or didn't like or anything else interesting.

Date of my Trip: _____/_____/_____   Place: _____

Picture of the Day

Details
Write about what you did, the best part of the day, what you saw, your favorite part of the day, what you liked or didn't like or anything else interesting.

Date of my Trip: _____/_____/_____   Place: _____

Picture of the Day

Details
Write about what you did, the best part of the day, what you saw, your favorite part of the day, what you liked or didn't like or anything else interesting.

Date of my Trip: _____/_____/_____ Place: _____

Picture of the Day

Details
Write about what you did, the best part of the day, what you saw, your favorite
part of the day, what you liked or didn't like or anything else interesting.

- -

- -

- -

- -

- -

- -

- -

- -

- -

- -

- -

- -

Date of my Trip: _____/_____/_____ Place: _____

Picture of the Day

Details
Write about what you did, the best part of the day, what you saw, your favorite part of the day, what you liked or didn't like or anything else interesting.

Date of my Trip: _____/_____/_____   Place: _____

Picture of the Day

Details
Write about what you did, the best part of the day, what you saw, your favorite part of the day, what you liked or didn't like or anything else interesting.

_____

_____

_____

_____

_____

_____

_____

_____

_____

_____

_____

_____

Date of my Trip: _____/_____/_____ Place: _____

Picture of the Day

Details
Write about what you did, the best part of the day, what you saw, your favorite part of the day, what you liked or didn't like or anything else interesting.

Date of my Trip: _____/_____/_____   Place: _____

Picture of the Day

Details
Write about what you did, the best part of the day, what you saw, your favorite part of the day, what you liked or didn't like or anything else interesting.

Date of my Trip: _____/_____/_____   Place: _____

Picture of the Day

Details
Write about what you did, the best part of the day, what you saw, your favorite part of the day, what you liked or didn't like or anything else interesting.

Date of my Trip: _____/_____/_____   Place: _____

Picture of the Day

Details
Write about what you did, the best part of the day, what you saw, your favorite part of the day, what you liked or didn't like or anything else interesting.

- -

- -

- -

- -

- -

- -

- -

- -

- -

- -

- -

- -

Date of my Trip: _____/_____/_____   Place: _____

Picture of the Day

Details
Write about what you did, the best part of the day, what you saw, your favorite part of the day, what you liked or didn't like or anything else interesting.

Date of my Trip: _____/_____/_____ Place: _____

Picture of the Day

Details
Write about what you did, the best part of the day, what you saw, your favorite part of the day, what you liked or didn't like or anything else interesting.

Date of my Trip: _____/_____/_____ Place: _____

Picture of the Day

Details
Write about what you did, the best part of the day, what you saw, your favorite part of the day, what you liked or didn't like or anything else interesting.

Date of my Trip: _____/_____/_____   Place: _____

Picture of the Day

Details

Write about what you did, the best part of the day, what you saw, your favorite part of the day, what you liked or didn't like or anything else interesting.

Date of my Trip: _____/_____/_____   Place: _____

Picture of the Day

Details

Write about what you did, the best part of the day, what you saw, your favorite part of the day, what you liked or didn't like or anything else interesting.

\- -

\- -

\- -

\- -

\- -

\- -

\- -

\- -

\- -

\- -

\- -

Date of my Trip: _____/_____/_____   Place: _____

Picture of the Day

Details
Write about what you did, the best part of the day, what you saw, your favorite part of the day, what you liked or didn't like or anything else interesting.

Date of my Trip: _____ / _____ / _____   Place: _____

Picture of the Day

Details
Write about what you did, the best part of the day, what you saw, your favorite part of the day, what you liked or didn't like or anything else interesting.

_____

_____

_____

_____

_____

_____

_____

_____

_____

_____

_____

Date of my Trip: _____/_____/_____   Place: _____

Picture of the Day

Details
Write about what you did, the best part of the day, what you saw, your favorite part of the day, what you liked or didn't like or anything else interesting.

Date of my Trip: _____/_____/_____   Place: _____

Picture of the Day

Details
Write about what you did, the best part of the day, what you saw, your favorite part of the day, what you liked or didn't like or anything else interesting.

Date of my Trip: _____/_____/_____   Place: _____

Picture of the Day

Details
Write about what you did, the best part of the day, what you saw, your favorite part of the day, what you liked or didn't like or anything else interesting.

Date of my Trip: _____/_____/_____   Place: _____

Picture of the Day

Details
Write about what you did, the best part of the day, what you saw, your favorite part of the day, what you liked or didn't like or anything else interesting.

- -

- -

- -

- -

- -

- -

- -

- -

- -

- -

- -

- -

Date of my Trip: _____/_____/_____ Place: _____

Picture of the Day

Details
Write about what you did, the best part of the day, what you saw, your favorite part of the day, what you liked or didn't like or anything else interesting.

_____

_____

_____

_____

_____

_____

_____

_____

_____

_____

_____

_____

Date of my Trip: _____/_____/_____   Place: _____

Picture of the Day

Details
Write about what you did, the best part of the day, what you saw, your favorite part of the day, what you liked or didn't like or anything else interesting.

Date of my Trip: _____/_____/_____   Place: _____

Picture of the Day

Details
Write about what you did, the best part of the day, what you saw, your favorite part of the day, what you liked or didn't like or anything else interesting.

Date of my Trip: _____/_____/_____   Place: _____

Picture of the Day

Details
Write about what you did, the best part of the day, what you saw, your favorite part of the day, what you liked or didn't like or anything else interesting.

- -
- -
- -
- -
- -
- -
- -
- -
- -
- -
- -
- -

Date of my Trip: _____/_____/_____   Place: _____

Picture of the Day

Details
Write about what you did, the best part of the day, what you saw, your favorite part of the day, what you liked or didn't like or anything else interesting.

_____

_____

_____

_____

_____

_____

_____

_____

_____

_____

_____

_____

Date of my Trip: _____/_____/_____   Place: _____

Picture of the Day

Details
Write about what you did, the best part of the day, what you saw, your favorite part of the day, what you liked or didn't like or anything else interesting.

- -

- -

- -

- -

- -

- -

- -

- -

- -

- -

- -

Date of my Trip: _____/_____/_____   Place: _____

Picture of the Day

Details
Write about what you did, the best part of the day, what you saw, your favorite part of the day, what you liked or didn't like or anything else interesting.

Date of my Trip: _____/_____/_____   Place: _____

Picture of the Day

Details
Write about what you did, the best part of the day, what you saw, your favorite part of the day, what you liked or didn't like or anything else interesting.

Date of my Trip: _____/_____/_____   Place: _____

Picture of the Day

Details
Write about what you did, the best part of the day, what you saw, your favorite part of the day, what you liked or didn't like or anything else interesting.

Date of my Trip: _____/_____/_____   Place: _____

Picture of the Day

Details
Write about what you did, the best part of the day, what you saw, your favorite part of the day, what you liked or didn't like or anything else interesting.

Date of my Trip: _____/_____/_____ Place: _____

Picture of the Day

Details
Write about what you did, the best part of the day, what you saw, your favorite part of the day, what you liked or didn't like or anything else interesting.

- -

- -

- -

- -

- -

- -

- -

- -

- -

- -

- -

- -

Date of my Trip: _____/_____/_____   Place: _____

Picture of the Day

Details
Write about what you did, the best part of the day, what you saw, your favorite part of the day, what you liked or didn't like or anything else interesting.

Date of my Trip: _____/_____/_____ Place: _____

Picture of the Day

Details
Write about what you did, the best part of the day, what you saw, your favorite part of the day, what you liked or didn't like or anything else interesting.

_____

_____

_____

_____

_____

_____

_____

_____

_____

_____

_____

_____

Date of my Trip: _____/_____/_____   Place: _____

Picture of the Day

Details
Write about what you did, the best part of the day, what you saw, your favorite part of the day, what you liked or didn't like or anything else interesting.

Date of my Trip: _____/_____/_____   Place: _____

Picture of the Day

Details
Write about what you did, the best part of the day, what you saw, your favorite part of the day, what you liked or didn't like or anything else interesting.

Date of my Trip: _____/_____/_____   Place: _____

Picture of the Day

Details
Write about what you did, the best part of the day, what you saw, your favorite part of the day, what you liked or didn't like or anything else interesting.

Date of my Trip: _____/_____/_____ Place: _____

Picture of the Day

Details
Write about what you did, the best part of the day, what you saw, your favorite part of the day, what you liked or didn't like or anything else interesting.

Date of my Trip: _____/_____/_____   Place: _____

Picture of the Day

Details

Write about what you did, the best part of the day, what you saw, your favorite part of the day, what you liked or didn't like or anything else interesting.

Date of my Trip: _____/_____/_____   Place: _____

Picture of the Day

Details
Write about what you did, the best part of the day, what you saw, your favorite part of the day, what you liked or didn't like or anything else interesting.

Date of my Trip: _____/_____/_____ Place: _____

Picture of the Day

Details
Write about what you did, the best part of the day, what you saw, your favorite part of the day, what you liked or didn't like or anything else interesting.

Date of my Trip: _____/_____/_____   Place: _____

Picture of the Day

Details
Write about what you did, the best part of the day, what you saw, your favorite part of the day, what you liked or didn't like or anything else interesting.

_____

_____

_____

_____

_____

_____

_____

_____

_____

_____

_____

_____

Need Another Blank Trips Journal?
Visit www.blankbooksnjournals.com

CPSIA information can be obtained
at www.ICGtesting.com
Printed in the USA
LVOW09s0345130418
573364LV00018B/594/P